Walkabout

"In Diane Sherman's debut collection, *Walkabout*, we are invited to go on an intimate, spiritual journey. In the beginning, an innocent child tries to deal with the pain incurred by her father's death. All of our senses are engaged as we walk with this child through chapters of her life; through a series of relationships that speak of love and betrayal; through self-doubt and temptation; through the rigors demanded by strenuous wilderness treks. Bravely facing every setback that empties her, Diane Sherman opens anew to possibility and transformation. She fills, and so do we. By the end of this book, her journey has become our own, and we return from these poems with greater wisdom and compassion. The title of her beautiful and haunting last poem, *Silver Weaver*, says it all."

Rose Black
author of *Clearing* and *Winter Light*

"Diane's words speak with a raw freshness that sinks in like gentle rain on soft ground in one poem, bursting into bright neon in the next. She weaves together that which is so personal into bridges of connection and insight that reach across this vastness of experience with provocative uncompromising candor. She not only reveals unspoken intimacies of her inner world, but leaves the reader feeling she has spied on ours as well, valiantly layering the mundane with the sublime, allowing us to savor this unpredictable, precious life anew."

Sarah Powers
author of *Insight Yoga*

"Diane's poems reveal a unique and particular inner landscape with fearless honesty. They show how the turn toward the inner life–even when difficult and painful–can lead to insight, strength, and healing. Diane gifts us with these poems by inviting us to take this turn, too, and to make ourselves fearlessly vulnerable, as she does, again and again, to the truth of our history and the truth of our life as it is now."

Cybèle Tomlinson
author of *Simple Yoga* and *Ayurveda Wisdom*

Walkabout

poems

Diane Sherman

ACKNOWLEDGMENTS

The author gratefully thanks the publications in which these poems first appeared, sometimes in different versions:

Alembic: "City Moment"
Diverse Voices Quarterly: "Undertow"
Pisgah Review: "Undertow"
The Cape Rock: "Meeting the Reader"
The Spokesman Review: "That Wild Thing"
                        "Beyond Barbed Wire"
Sanskrit Literary-Arts Magazine: "Meeting the Reader"

ISBN: 0615482457
ISBN-13: 9780615482453

Cover Photograph: Diane Sherman
Cover Design: Diane Sherman
Author Photograph: Matthew Carden
Book Design: Diane Sherman

Printed in the United States of America

For Erez

CONTENTS

Walkabout

The title of this book is inspired by the Aboriginal rite of passage that adolescent boys undertake to become men in the eyes of society. For a period of up to six months they wander alone in the bush, making their way through a spiritual journey and returning to their clan with more maturity, wisdom, and self-guidance.

In many Western cultures we lack initiation rites for our youth, and tend to amble into our twenties and thirties, trying to find our way as best we can with little guidance as to how to access inner wisdom. We are often told to follow rules, regurgitate already chewed on answers, and buck up and follow along. How do we find our true passion, our true calling, unless we listen deeply within?

This book is an offering from my own curvy path: challenging initiations, the feeling of being lost with no oars on a stormy ocean, obstacles to tackle along the way and ultimately the transformative power of maturation through life's trials. No one in life escapes difficulty. We lose those we love, we age and lose our youthful bounce, we make mistakes and hurt people unconsciously, we grasp and cling to what we think we want and do our damndest to avoid that which we feel most uncomfortable with. Often, our discomfort points to possible edges of transformation.

This is my first collection of poetry. I offer you these poems as glimpses into the places we stumble, pick ourselves up, take another step along the path and hopefully enjoy some of the journey.

I wish you inspired living, to do what you love, to love who you're with, and to somehow make this planet a better place by offering your gifts to the world. Blessings along the way.

—Diane Sherman

SKID MARKS

Walkabout

I walk in his funeral procession—
black velvet dress with puffy sleeves,
Mary Jane patent leather shoes,
white bobby socks fringed with lace.

I stroll through campus, Wordsworth tucked
under my arm, rust-colored leaves
dangle on dry branches. I see him
riding the white horse,
wearing a black cowboy hat, holding
it on his head with his right hand.
He gallops to my side, asks
about school, if I'm in love, how
I like the snow. Just then, the wind
off the lake pierces my chest, and he's gone.

The Speed of Life

Gray and limp, it lies
lifeless in our front yard.
Just this morning
it batted its tail,
dashed up trees, buried nuts.

I see it happen, the run
and chase, the catch,
legs scrambling,
life clinging to itself.
Last breath comes faster
than I can dial my mother.
A bite, a snap. Ragdoll
in my dog's mouth.

She prances across the street,
tail up, prize hangs from clenched jaws.

How quickly life leaves us.
One last breath, a heart attack
in London's Heathrow, shells on ground,
bomb blast in Jerusalem markets,
an earthquake in Haiti.

How long it takes the living
to recover.

After the Bite

Jimmy glides in murky water,
kelp hands on calf, shark
bite in meaty flesh. My thirteen
year old heart beats for his ocean
eyes, an older man—fourteen.

Sandy hair rocks and rolls
down his forehead, his mango lips
the ones I want to suck and lick.
We play hide and seek,
punch and kick, push and shove.
He loves me, loves me not,
rose petals drop to ground.
He loves me,
until he loves me not.

Spin the bottle kiss, a ghost
after the bite, flailing legs,
arms, shady waters, great
white shark, Jaws full screen
and wham, whack,
gotcha, ha ha ha ha,
I hate you ocean eyes,
soft skin, I love you
not.

White Sheets

I wore white sheets at the toga party,
before I slipped into stiff,
cotton ones on his metal
dorm bed. His roommates'
snores drifted through thin walls,
beer-heavy brains on flat pillows.

I was a Catholic girl. They'd
told me not to travel the canyon
between silky thighs where
power surged.

I'd only heard about it, talked
about it, glistening bodies
rolling and rubbing
their way to rapture.

So after his poking
and prodding, searching for
the entrance, after the quick
convulsion and guttural sigh,
he rolled off me and slumbered.

Deflowered, I lay on his bed,
a trace of my schoolgirl self.
I slunk down the hall,
found my own pillow
and cried. I'd never wear
those white sheets again.

Grinding Stone

I
It's been in the kitchen drawer for two decades,
next to the spatula and can opener—
a present he gave her for her first apartment,
just big enough for a single bed and a dot
of a kitchen table on Stockton Street.

When he showed her how to use it,
he emphasized it had two sides:
fine and coarse.
He wet the stone, held it in his left hand;
his right hand held the butcher knife.
Swoosh, the blade back and forth,
wrist spinning crazy eights,
the sound of metal grinding.

In college she'd rolled her hips
for him. He said she was the one,
then moved to another continent.
On thin sheathes he wrote her
from a Philippine village,
told her he wanted to be a priest.
She saved all his letters.

Five years later she decided
he was the one.

II
A coarse and fine side.
She became the coarse side
and ground them down,
churned them up,
spit them out on shore.

Skid Marks

You could say it was over
before the ambulance came,
before Highland Hospital,
before they told me it would take
six months to walk after the cast.

I'd said goodbye to you
many times in my head.
Goodbye to the daily
pot habit, the pack-a-day
smokes, the porn addiction.
Goodbye to the acid trips,
to your dingy frayed
t-shirts and baggy pants,
to the buzz of your clippers
on my pubic hair.

Yes, that Ash Wednesday
when the steel blue
Camaro skidded
and screeched, black tire marks
left as proof, that day
when you flew hawk over top,
me kick ball to goal post,
that day I knew it was finished
for good. *Fait accompli.*

Once paramedics stretched me
out, scissors severed
favorite brown velvet dress,
morphine dripped into veins,
I knew I'd be eating Jell-O
from hospital trays, receiving
cards and yellow roses.

I just didn't know how long
it would take to rinse
you out of my blood.

Can't You Imagine?

I told him on our first date,
over *injera* and hot Ethiopian
peppers and peas.
It was on the table.
No point in a second date
if he couldn't accept it. Not to mention
I already felt too old. He called
me for a second and a third.
Would he change his mind? How
could he give up something
like that? He said he loved me
that much, wanted to be
with me. The salt sting
came later.

Can't you imagine?
he'd begin, *the three of us,*
our own little unit, running
through spring gardens, baking
bread, playing gin rummy?
Can't you imagine
her running home
with her first
finger-painting?
Can't you?

Heartland Home

They reel her back to corn cob
land, where summer's sweat lodge
sits you on a porch, limbs limp.
She thrashes on the end of the line,
tail swishing back and forth, unable
to unfasten the family hook.

It's their time now. She and her
ninety-two-year-old mother, frail as a spider
web in winter. Clouds of gray puff
through tired lungs. Her feet gnarled,
toes twisted, raspberry tips curled
one over the other.

The house is littered with papers,
photos, dirty ashtrays, times they left
her alone. She remembers how Santa
and his reindeer came and how she
never seemed to see them, not knowing
her older brother was throwing stones
on the roof.

She sits with her mother and paints
her nails, lights her cigarettes.
She'll watch thunderstorms
roll by and soak the homeland.

Arriving Spokane

I am neither here nor there,
30,000 feet above ground.
My cat sits in a black bag under
the seat in front of me. By my side
two business geeks talk distribution
cycles and marketing plans.
I read the same lines of my novel
over and over.

As I wait for the tiny-stall bathroom,
a former California guy asks me about my boots.
Keens, I say. *Just bought them for the cold
weather.* He tells me his ex-wife had a hard
time when they first came to Spokane. I wonder
if that's why they're divorced, and if that will
be my fate.

By the time we pass Mt. Bachelor, the movers
will unload the truck. By the time I arrive,
the truck will be empty.

He gives me her number, scrawled on the back
of an old business card. *Call her, she'll be happy
to talk with you.* I smile and look down,
tuck the card in my wallet.

DRIZZLE IN THE HOLLOW

Why Can't I Find the Right Train?

The train station hums, voices
bellow *chai chai chai*. Green and gold
saris bustle across platforms.
Everyone is going somewhere.

My hand shakes as I hand
the *chai wallah* my wadded-up
rupee for a short cup.
I search for something familiar,
another foreign face, signs
for trains, a line to stand in.

Resentment has taken root
like crabgrass. How do I leave you
behind? Why can't I find the right train?

My stomach grumbles, muscles
ache from lugging overstuffed bags
through pinhole streets. We pass
child beggars with outstretched
hands, leg stumps, blind eyes.

Black-haired men push and shove
at the station window, throw down rupees
for a ticket. I rub the one in my pocket
like a worry bead.

On My Street

Snug up against the freeway pass, he sleeps
on sheets of cardboard in a sleeping bag.
Overhead, cars hustle to work, to home,
to home, to work.

In the morning he drives his cart
down the center of the street, bends and stoops,
collects bottles from blue recycling bins.

Like leaves in fall, debris litters the street—
yellow Post-It notes, tinfoil, plastic bags
that didn't make it to the giant truck.

Squatting, I clean up drifting rubbish in front
of my house. And I nearly pick it up, the paper towel
stuck to the mound, but my nose gets a whiff
just in time. My hand recoils.

Who does *this* belong to?

White Lies and Mirrors

I'm sober, clean, in recovery.
We believed him.

Then his lover left us
the message:
He's been gone
two days,
took the dog,
left a butcher knife
in the bathtub.
I'm scared.

Buddha belly man
on the run, demon
shadows chasing.

His lover's words slur
through the telephone.
He tried to kill me.
Faint winter light
streams through
my kitchen window.

We didn't notice
until after we knew.

Family Portrait

His summer days begin with vodka
tonics, ice cubes clink in glass.
Tiny pearls of sweat drip to the table.
Mornings steam hot by the Chesapeake Bay.

White cotton shirt falls off skinny
shoulders of his wire hanger wife.
Aprons double tie around her waist.
When she speaks her bird voice
is high and shrill.

By noon he's had two or three,
slurs his words and shouts at the wife.

He dotes on his adopted thirteen-year-old,
buys her black lace lingerie
and see-through nighties.

She can't wait to open her gifts.

Catholic Education

Our teacher blows up the condom
and bats it around the classroom.
A volleyball flying in all directions.

How many people think masturbation is unnatural?

My hand shoots up, sure I hold
the majority view. I mean,
I don't really know what it means.
In my pleated skirt and knee-highs,
I follow the rules—

don't touch yourself 'down there'
you'll go to Hell

Only two other hands are raised.
Blood creeps up to my face,
strawberry red and hot.

Why do you think masturbation is unnatural?
he asks as he approaches.

I sink in my seat,
eyes fixed on the scarred
wood in front of me.

Miss Sherman?

Drizzle in the Hollow

At my thirtieth high school reunion classmates talk
about their children, show pictures of college
students at UCLA, Stanford, Brown. They brag
how their seventh grader won the science fair
contest, how their teenage daughter has
purple hair, a pierced navel and wants
to go to art school.

I show pictures of our dog, her first birthday
party, her boyfriend Tank and how they play
tug of war with a bone.

I've been told a million times I'd make a great
mom. But can't they see my drizzle in the hollow?
Wet diapers, midnight feedings, carting
to hockey and ballet? Can they see my husband's
thirty-something cells explode with longing?

Twitching and Swaying

My friend's newborn
slumps over my shoulder.
I rock side to side.

As I sway, he presses his floppy
head against my neck.
His miniature fingers and toes twitch,
random spurts of energy move
tiny legs and arms,
tiny explosions of the soul.

I am in love.

I've never really wanted a baby of my own,
but in this instant I do.
The reasons to not have one
suddenly gone. Some other version
of myself stands here in the kitchen.

My mind flashes 20 questions.
*Could my forty-six-year-old body
make a baby?
Should I start now?
How old will I be
when he's fifteen?
Am I crazy?
Or should I just babysit?*

I return to the twitching,
the cooing, the swaying.
Peach fuzz head snug
in the nape of my neck.

You Can't Win a Rodeo Sittin'
in the Bucking Chute

Spaghetti noodle necks snap and sway, spines swivel,
chaps and cowboy boots fly left and right atop ball-bound bulls.
The MC hoots and hollers, *You can't win a rodeo sittin' in the
bucking chute.*

The rider's right hand holds on for every extra second,
black bull snorts and bucks, hind feet kick up Wyoming dirt.
Then *BAM*, cowboy's flung off, scrambles towards pen railing.

I sit safely in the bleachers, popcorn bag in hand. *Wahoo!*
we yell for each rider. I imagine myself racing around barrels
atop a chestnut mare, reigns in hand, cowboy boots kicking
faster, faster, and me holding my hat
so it doesn't fly as I race to the finish line.

Not bad, not bad at all, he chimes from his booth,
twenty three seconds for that pretty little lady there.

We are waiting

for gray summer clouds to pass,
for sun to become a permanent resident,
not just a visiting friend.

We are waiting to wear wide-brimmed hats
and slather on sunscreen, don white cotton
skirts that tickle ankles.

We are waiting to sip mint lemonade on the porch
and watch joggers trot by, some pushing baby carriages,
others with a dog at the end of a leash.

We are waiting to watch shirtless teenage boys
drip summer sweat and dribble
basketballs from hoop to hoop.

We are waiting for the pit in my stomach
to dissolve, the stickiness of grief
to melt away.

We are waiting for this new place
to feel like home.

River Runs

They zip zap zag
through branches
arched to river
rocks roll
boulders bound
puppy play pounce
rabbit legs
hop hop hop

it's morning time

sniff, scratch snarf
Who was here?
What did they do?
I'll leave my scent, too
river runs wild
towards Oregon
rapids churn
thoughts stir

put one foot
in front of the other,
Spokane—
Children of the Sun

Who was here?
What did they do?

run wild, run out
listen to wind,
river, sun pulse
warm on back

Children of the Sun
where are you now?

Rinse & Spit

I talked about liposuction with my dentist yesterday. My new
dentist, not the one I'd been going to for twenty years, the one
who always talked about sex, asked if I was getting any and with
whom. I tried not to say much to this ex-smoker, still Catholic,
Bush-supporting Republican. We had a truce on politics, and
since he held the drill I said nothing. How much can a person
say in the dentist's chair, mouth pried open, clamps and cotton
filling gaps, an occasional chance to rinse and spit?

*Did I tell you I quit smoking? Gained twenty pounds, but hey, that's
better than smoking, huh?* I heard about his kids, when they were
in grade school, high school, then college. Suddenly the girl
was engaged. He told me when his mother died, when his
wife left him, then came back, that he'd had a heart attack
and was eating more kale and chard. Each visit a peg in the
documentary of his life.

I'd been crossing the Bay Bridge year after year to see this man
my entire adult life. All the fillings and crowns in my mouth
were his. When I made the decision to leave him, or try to, I
gave myself an out. I told myself I would just *try* my husband's
dentist, a woman, who is only five minutes from our house. But
I felt I was cheating, scorning a lover, choosing someone else.
So I did what lovers do when things get awkward.

I just didn't call him.

A Married Woman

Her hands glide through clear water,
sweep her thighs, head turns left-right,
left-right from the swivel of the hips, mouth
sucks air like a guppy.

At the bottom of the pool, she sees
the long black line reminding her to stay
in her lane, then the T shape letting her know
she will need to turn before she crashes.

She met her long-haired lover
in hotels with scratchy sheets
and polyester pillows. How free
she felt, rinsed in his essence,
her fingers charged with longing.
Or love?

In late August he told her
it was over. He was in love
with someone else.

She elongates her arms, stretches
chest open as her hands slide through
ripples. At the bottom of the pool
she sees her shimmering shadow.

New Delhi Dreams

They slither on scorching Delhi pavement
from one hotel lobby to another, to rest on posh
couches, two twenty-something wilting lilies,
before the bell captain says, *You cannot sit here
unless you are a hotel guest.*

Cobblestones sizzle underfoot as they inhale
jasmine incense mixed with rotting garbage.
They slip through alleyways,
sputtering discontent at each other
while searching for a room.

At home, with maps spread on kitchen tables,
there were no flies and filth, sticky sweat
trickling down necks. No water-drenched
sheets at sweltering midnight, no incessant
tick-tick of the whirling overhead fan.

No. Saffron saris fluttered, balmy nights
begged mango *lassis,* holy men in loin-
cloths bathed and prayed in the river.

Horns honk, rickshaws clatter, slumber
is a distant cousin. Across the hall,
in Western-style toilet, rat hands
paddle for dear life. She chooses
the two-step squat in the other stall.

They're no longer sure why they came.
To see temples, eat curry, sit with holy men
by the river? To come home changed, more wise,
more content? They count the days now, dream
of cool winds from the Pacific, spotless bathrooms
and queen-sized beds.

In the morning she tells the front desk:
There was a rat in the toilet upstairs, sir.
Oh yes, Madam, yes. So many rats, so many rats.

UNDERTOW

Undertow

I'm supposed to get my period
today, according to my iPhone
period tracker. All indicators on target,
tender breasts, irritable, the doom and gloom
chemical cocktail, a tsunami of tears. It all
slams up my husband's shore, hits broadside,
a tidal wave he has no idea how to ride.
Belly flat on board, arms flail, he paddles
hard, tries to stand, the white cap on his
heels, so close he yells over the roar.
He tells me it isn't so, reality kaleidoscoped
in a fun house, chemicals gone array.
Who is this person in front of him,
this ragdoll heap, snot-blowing
forty-something woman?

He wants to snap me back to normal,
back to calm Caribbean seas, but the swell
is well underway, dangerous undertow.
Red lights flash up and down the shore:
Abort, Abort, the siren wails.
Abort, Abort, wait for this to pass.
Say nothing and duck.

Discontent

She sashays in, Discontent,
a drama queen with fedora hat.
She carries linen hanky in velvet
pocket to dab drips of malaise.
Fingers cling to lists of disgruntles.

Bliss, she is sure, is on the other side
of the planet. *Oh poor me,*
she cues her audience.
Poor me, it's too hot, too cold,
too busy, too quiet...

The list, an Amazonian Boa constrictor,
chokes her pleasure. Blind
to her own doing she flings
feathered Boa over shoulder,
pounds explosive fists on table.
Listen to me, listen to me,
she screams. Her audience
now deaf to her pleas.

Once-attentive patrons roll
and unroll playbills
in hands, cough, and turn their
gaze sideways. No amount
of pounding and shouting
lures them back.

Altoid Dessert

I want a glass of wine
to partner my meal of lightly
battered catfish and pickled beet salad.
But the headache to follow
beats the longing out of me. The throb
over my right eye that will last all night
into day. I order water instead,
ice cubes clink in my glass.
It's no thin singing wine glass,
the kind I hold by the stem,
swirl ruby liquid, inhale the bouquet.

There will be no dessert either.
Irritability soars with intake,
the white crystal, methamphetamine
to my system.

Dessert menu?

Without looking
at one another
we chant *no.*

No dessert.
No sugar.
No cookies.
No ice cream.
No.

My husband, a semi-willing
prisoner of war on sugar.
He knows I'll cheat if he does.

We ask for the check.

In the car I dig in the glove compartment
for the red and white tin and offer him
a slim, white mint.

Wedding Band

Stone-cold floor, miniature windows, two sinks, two sets of plates. Black-hatted rabbi sits on worn leather couch, eyes cloudy with age, hand limp when I shake it. His wife, my husband's grandmother, delivers us from room to room, points to sun-faded photos which hang on cream-colored walls. In these she stands smooth-faced and sturdy among her brood.

We step through her door two days before the wedding, not ours, my brother-in-law's. She mistakes us for bride and groom.

When will you *marry? Will it be in the States? Will I be invited?*

I cover my platinum wedding band with my right hand, shift side to side. My husband says, *Let's focus on the wedding at hand.*

It's not important that she know, his mother says, sitting in her own stone-floor apartment four blocks away. *She won't understand why she wasn't invited. Perhaps she'll never have to know.*

I keep my wedding band covered. She and I stand next to each other looking at sun-faded photos, ex-Catholic yogi and Orthodox Jew.

Blood Diamond

This is not a blood diamond—
it was my grandmother's.
We didn't send money to rebels
in Angola, Congo, or Liberia.

The diamond sparkles magic
crystal on my finger—I ride
its beams to the moon and back
through peacock skies.

Across the globe, tiny fingers sift
through dirt for magic rocks, children
guard children with rifles and machetes.
Clean hands clutch pregnant
cash bags, abandon bodies in ditches.
Wars rage along borders.

I wear my ring and see Granny sitting
at her vanity, coating lips crimson.
Did a child find this rock?
I wear my ring and wonder if someone died.

Twin Pillars

We mingle, bare backs
and long sleeves, share
chicken satay, kebobs
and pita filled pockets.
Photographers mill among
us, flash lights at friends
and relatives, some who
won't speak to each other.

Leaves in wind, we are gathered
up under the satin canopy,
handful of family to witness white
lace and rings, prayers and vows.

Women on the right, men on the left,
my husband flanks his brother, the groom.

If she knew, she wouldn't stand
next to me, his grandmother,
mother of five. She's eaten dairy and meat
on separate plates for nearly eighty years,
lived through wars. She always asks him,
When will you marry?
When will you marry?

Two years now I've covered
the platinum band on my left
hand. Me, the non-Hebrew speaking,
ham-and-cheese eating, former Catholic.

She wraps her arm around my
waist, we stand shoulder to
shoulder, twin pillars under the *chuppah*.

Shabbat

Cold stone, cold feet.
Cold stone, cold floor.
We wait for hot water.
The boiler's red light offers hope.

Electric teapot clicks on and off.
I cup a hot mug in my hands
and stand in front of electric heater
in the center of the living room.

Rain pelts windows,
pours down
slant, sheets in wind.
Large spruce
tree rocks outside.
Winged branches
tremble.

We huddle together,
four penguins
on a couch.

Shabbat.

Stores closed. Restaurants
shut. Car engines dormant,
cell phones asleep, computers
at rest. Nowhere to go.

I search the hall for slippers.

We fire up TV and watch a movie,
wait for the growl of our stomachs,
any reason to lift off the couch.

Across town,
black hats walk Jerusalem streets.
Clickety clack,
boots on cobblestone,
long black coats.

Sinners with open umbrellas
weave among them.

The Fifth Car

My right eye throbs, I have no Tylenol and I'm behind
the steering wheel. I got this headache in traffic, or from
traffic. Cars honk, dodge left, right, blinker, no blinker.

Snarled traffic parking lot. I take the nearest freeway exit
and see him on the corner. Rumpled plaid shirt, black baseball
cap, his hands hold a sign—*Anything helps, even a smile.* I'm stuck
at a red light. He's walking my way. I'm the fifth car in line.

My back aches and I'm heading home to my down comforter
and warm bed. I wish he would turn around and walk the other
way. He passes the first two cars, their windows rolled up tight.
Then the third, then the fourth.

My ten-year-old Nissan is wedged between a black Mercedes
and a beige Lexus. I stare at the license plate in front of me
hoping this man will disappear. As he steps forward my chest
constricts. I find my hand digging for any green bill in my bag.
As the light turns, I roll down my window, place a five-dollar
bill in his palm.

The Lexus behind me honks.

Autumn Dinner

He tells her at the Italian restaurant,
red and white checkered tablecloths,
stiff wooden chairs.

If I were perfect for you, I'd be in love with you.

Crimson leaves blaze against sapphire
sky. Wind sings through balding
branches, last leaves flutter.

Head down, she stares at her pasta,
picks through red sauce, stabs
her fork into bits of meat. Her cheeks
burn. Winter bends around the corner.

City Moment

She's missing three front teeth,
the stench of her clothes wafts
perfume as I walk by, chapped
fingers reach my way.

Can you spare some money for food?

I wear black velvet,
Pashmina wraps my shoulders,
a gold Buddha head peers
out from the side of my purse.
My white-haired mother's arm
linked in mine.

The City whirls blonde
long hair, black leather, tight jeans,
cell phones ring and text,
I'll meet you on the corner,
by the pub, next to the hotel.
Bright lights scream
Buy something in neon pinks.
Red lipsticks, blue eyeliners,
slinky cocktail dresses,
crinkly spring raincoats.
New look, new life.

Can you spare some money for food?

My throat clogs. I walk by
tightening the wrap of my shawl.
My hand doesn't reach into Buddha
purse, my own cupboards filled
with black beans and rice, Coho
salmon, asparagus, strawberries.

How did you lose your teeth?
Do you have children? A husband?
Where is your mother? When
did you last shower?

We step through mahogany
doors, the usher hands us a playbill
and we find our places.

CUTTINGS ON THE FLOOR

Muse

Wings of ideas tremble through gray skies, squawk in my brain.
Flawless poems roam in my head while walking the dog
by the river. Gurgling thoughts spin to slush before pen reaches
open page. By then my flock has flown south, no word or poem
in sight.

Question marks waltz in my head. How many galaxies
are there? Why do people hate? How can people kill with no
remorse? What's the secret of motherhood? Is there a god?

I make black Russian tea in a red teapot, stir in a teaspoon of
honey, splash of cream. I nuzzle the dog, scratch the cat's chin
as I meander to my chair, chasing yesterday's life
to put on a page.

Meeting the Reader

They don't all spill out like foamy cream
from the top of a milk bottle.
Some are stuck in caves or secret
crevices, you need a pick and shovel
to dig them up, and even then you wonder
what you've found—fool's gold
or the real thing. Extracting gems
takes years of hard labor, extensive
time travel, mashing and mar.
Once found they must be tumbled,
rolled, polished so their natural shine
glows and they are ready.
Ready to meet their reader, the one,
two, or perhaps thousands who
will roll them again on their lips,
in their ears, on the couch,
in bed, alone or next to a lover.
Listen to this, they will say
and the other
will close her eyes
and listen.

Sunset Trail

The trail circles you up
towards the sky and opens
its arms to the city below.
An eagle's view atop a rocky road.

I slog lead legs up the incline,
heart pumps, a loud drumbeat.
I mush on, a dog with a mission.
Sky blushes rose, city lights flicker.

Atop the hill a bench beckons
rest here. I sit and wait for my breath.
Then she starts her blushing.
The coquettish sky turns pink, bats
blue eyes. Cheeks turn crimson,
then hot pants pink. She simmers turmeric,
cinnamon and clove. Spicy lover, sky blazes red.
Her city suitor below flashes diamonds up
her way. They dance, the two, tango
and sway until she cools her evening flame.

Cuttings on the Floor

I have thin, fine hair
like a four-year-old,
dirty blonde, wispy
flyaway hair. I'm always
searching for product
to give volume and
shine. I wish for thick,
lustrous wavy hair spilling down
my back. Italian, Israeli,
Jewish hair, kinky, curly,
wild, tied-in-a-bun-on-my-head hair.
A handful of curls to grab ahold
of at the nape of the neck,
pull my head back, white skin
exposed to warm tongues, fresh bites.

No, mine is wet rat
ponytail, slicked back,
severely smoothed across skull.

Every two years I cut
it off, go sassy short,
use product to stand up
the backside. It's the kind
of haircut my mother
calls "trendy, searching
for something."

The minute I cut it, I start
to grow it out. I always believe
it will grow in thick and wavy
this time. But the same blonde
wisps appear and fly away
and I land in my hairdresser's chair.

Cut it off.
Again.

Yoga Cleanse

I dream of peanut butter and raspberry jam
spread thick on rye bread packed with sunflower
seeds and spelt flakes, a tall latte to wash
it down while lounging on the couch with the dog.

Instead I sip fennel-ginger tea and eat
bowls of mung bean rice *dahl*
with asparagus and kale.

My husband sits across the table,
stuffs a bagel full of dark leg chicken
meat, pickles and hot peppers.

How long does it last?
Seven days.
At least I can have figs.

It's day one. I wonder when I'll cheat
and how.

I open kitchen cupboards and stare
at Wheat Thins and pasta, almonds
and cashews. The Havarti cheese
in the fridge beckons.

Perfect Pen

I'm always looking for the perfect pen.
A pen that flows, glides, slips
evenly across the white plane.
We'll tango together, sweep the stage,
hear the *Milonga's* beat—two-four time.
I'll be coupled with my perfect pen
as it pivots and tilts, taps out thoughts
one after another. It will dissolve differences
between pen, paper, hand; hand and arm,
arm and brain, brain and thought.

The perfect pen erases laundry lists,
sashays with me into the moment's tempo,
rich and round. When I write with it
you will feel the chill of winter in the floorboards,
smell the butternut squash baking in the oven.

THAT WILD THING

Beyond barbed wire

security guards and double doors,
we sit on green mats inside and breathe.
Tattoos spill down their forearms
onto palms in downward facing dog.
Blue dragons circle ankles.
Demons nip at heels.

On slippery sticky mats we stand,
warriors, wings outstretched,
feet spread wide. The tallest one
has thirty more to go inside,
cell too small for his broad shoulders,
blue arms to reach to sky.

Out past these doors I'm shackled
to my lists, to my clock. I scurry
from this to that, hoping for a break,
wondering if I'm late, am I making
someone wait?

Back inside, in warrior two, their man
strong legs begin to quiver. *This was harder
than we thought.*

Together we breathe in and out,
eyes closed, fists unfurled,
bones yield to earth.

High Tibet

There is no escape. No helicopter,
airplane, train, bus, or taxi. No escape
from plodding along, one footstep at a time
through snow-crusted peaks close
enough to heaven to whisper to God.

No escape from the monkey
mind swinging from branch to branch,
craving this, avoiding that. Cravings come
in shotgun rounds: hot buttered French bread,
sautéed kale, gingered carrots,
cozy bed, steamy shower.

No escape on high plateau, wide
turquoise sky. Flags flutter, sing
prayers to the valley. Red robed
monks, shaved heads, spin prayer
wheels, *om mani padme hum, hail
to the jewel in the lotus flower.*
No escape.

When death takes a soul, the Lama
hacks arms, legs, hands, feet. Mixes
body parts with *tsampa*, lays it down
on parched earth for the swarming
black cloud of vultures above. Alms for
the birds. Sky burial. Bones left to bleach
in wasteland sun.

No escaping my sandbag legs,
duct-taped boots, the eye patch
I wear to calm the scratched
cornea, my almost empty water bottle
and parched throat. Nor can I
slink away from my dread
that I'll become bleached bones
on the plateau before I reach the answer.

That Wild Thing

I sit at my desk,
calendar in hand,
and wonder about life
with no schedule.

Don't we all want to know
that part of ourselves
with no meetings,
no deadlines,
no clocks?
That wild part
free of thank-you notes,
shopping lists,
laundry,
cleaning,
diapers?

It's where the lion runs
below Sahara sun,
yellow mane ripples,
breeze strokes his face.
Wild beasts move from the snarl
of their stomach, the ache
in their bones.

To roll in grass, purr, growl, play,
find our own grace.
Isn't it what our bones and marrow
call for from the jungle within?

Not a Catholic Anymore

Do this in memory of me.
Why did he say this
when I didn't even know his name?
This was before I figured out
he was speaking for someone else:
the one who cured the sick,
fed the hungry, comforted the poor.
The mystery man whose mother
was a virgin, whose father was God.
How could my seven-year-old brain
wrap itself around those facts?

And why were all the priests men?

Confession made my legs quiver.
My mind spun as I approached the dark closet.
Should I tell the priest I was mad at my mother?
I didn't walk the dog? That I drew a picture
of my math teacher and hung her
by the cord from the window?

I can't remember what I said.
I remember the rapid heartbeat,
confusion, sweaty palms. Why
did I have to confess when all I'd done
was try to be a good girl?

Now I'd have things to confess,
real sins, but it's too late.
I'm not a Catholic anymore.

Father's Silence

We stroll on snowy ground,
wool coat and blue scarf
wrapped around him. Bare
branches stretch from curb
to curb. He is silent. His hat
tilts down at an angle.
Frosted leaves crunch
under our soles. I loop
my arm through his,
match my step to his
gait. I wonder why he rarely
speaks now.

Has his wife talked
him into silence after
forty years of marriage?

The light is fading.
It's four p.m. Blue sky
turns gray, we nudge
our scarves up high
around our necks.

Dappled hands
sport brown and purple
spots, dry flecks sit
snowflake on his scalp.
His shoulders slope toward
frozen earth.

We turn back toward
the house, arms still
entwined. Time to
rest, lie down.
Night is coming.

Neila

We laugh, two hyenas
at a den feast, bellies
tired from so much
rolling. Eyes full of laughing tears.
We melt to puddles of ourselves.

She's winter's bear now,
tucked away, no easy inroads.
Lungs blackened by soot and tar.

I still see her before she withered,
her lion mane, her soft eyes
sitting on pomegranate cheeks.

Raven Heart

Your wing beat deafens canyons
in red rock desert.

Wing beat.
Heart beat.

Heart beat of God
as you fly by time and again—
big   black   raven   bird,
raven heart.

Still,
quiet,
hot midday sun,
baked clay earth,
rocks crackle beneath
my boots. I lope from pine
to pine, chasing shade
at high noon.

I forget about God's heart beat
and there You are again
clapping it out loud for me.

Quiet.
Still.
Cars hum in the distance,
miles away, out of sight.

Sun blazes.
White cotton candy clouds
appear in afternoon.
I lie on my back and watch
the parade of melting faces.

In the distance,
thunder.

Grace

She stands tall and proud.
Uncombed yellow hair
flies in the wind,
licks the blue sky,
dances haywire
on her bulbous head.

She bows and butts
saffron head to green carpet.
Heart-shaped hands
wave hello like a queen
passing in a car.

She's mature, full and round.
Her face droops south,
seeds bulge from her forehead.

Day after day, she stands
in my garden, aging with grace.

LIBERATION ROAD

Liberation Road

I search for a summer dress in the overstuffed
thrift shop. Pants and dresses bulge from round
racks, long poles. Shoes drip off shelves, belts hang
dreadlock from hooks. I want something that won't
emphasize my pubescent breasts. Secretly I eye
the patent leather six-inch-high fuck-me shoes.
I try them on. Too small.

In the corner, red and black thigh-high
stripper boots catch my gaze. Four-inch heels,
lace-up fronts. I wonder who wore these
and if she pole danced.

I glance sideways before I pull them from the shelf.
The pale young woman behind the counter looks
my way. *Check these out,* I announce, wanting
her to know I'm just looking.

Too small again. That's when I see the other
boots, pointy toes, three-inch heels. The boots
I will wear only to dance for *him,* black hose
and garter belt, padded push-up bra.

Red Ride

The warnings are out there:
Don't do it, don't get involved,
stay clear of temptation. Best
let growling beasts alone.
Sure we'll end up two flies
on windshields, mothers,
friends wag fear fingers in our faces.

It rumbles red between legs,
surges up our thighs into our hearts—
beating sparrow wings. Our hands
in leather grip tight, throttle revs
engine and we sail, glide
on blacktop, wheels spin,
chrome glistens dinnertime
pinks and blues. Jackets billow
and flap, summer wind licks
our necks. Gold fields flank
roving ribbon road. We lean into
curves, shoulders tip to ground.

Our fingers grip and turn, we kick
it in, ride, two blue herons
surfing wind currents,
wings spread wide.

Yellow Canyons

Meet me
in yellow canyons
where hawks glide
on air currents
and free fall to earth.
Free fall with me.

First Day

Have you ever watched
the squirrels
run the highways
of branches,
squabbling in their
chirpy way?

I have.
I wonder what
they're saying.

Miles below,
in squirrel terms,
the dogwoods bloom.
White petals
drift to earth
like snowflakes.
Birds call out
their morning song,
flutter wings
against the wind.

It is my first day married.
I sit still, and listen.

Slipping Out

Death rattled Granny's hospital bed
as she lay on prickly sheets with tubes
up her nose, skin drooping off bones.
She'd suffered so many strokes
her own daughters stopped counting.

Death rattled and drummed,
knocked and pounded year after year.
One night she glided out with the guest,
slid away from this world of scratchy sheets,
tubes and hospital gowns. Free at last
to float and soar.

Silver Weaver

She travels
the inner perimeter.

Counter clockwise.

Each silver thread
fastened precisely
at the corner.
The fabric of her
home, stronger
with each turn.

Morning gold
lights her chocolate,
bulbous body.

She is weaver, builder,
homemaker, hunter.

Steadily, she turns
the wheel of time.

THANK YOU & NOTES

Thank You...

Thank you, Erez, for your constant support, love, and encouragement. This book would not exist without you.

Thank you, Mom and Dad, for encouraging me to be my best self.

Rose, I bow deeply to you. Your friendship, mentoring, and editing were quintessential ingredients for this book. Thank you for all the time, love, and energy you put into this project.

Ofer, what can I say? You are the younger brother I never had. Thanks for making me laugh so hard in life!

Thank you Cybèle for sharing so much of the inner life together. You help me catch flashing bits of wisdom.

Sarah, thank you for being such an inspirational teacher in my life. Deep bow.

To my dear friends who've listened to my poems, read them with a tender ear, I thank you.

To my yoga students who have inspired me to live as authentically as I can.

To my fellow dancers, THANK YOU for our movement in and around each other, breathing in, breathing out. Always learning, always grateful.

To each reader, thank you for taking the time to read this book.

Notes

The poem "Walkabout" is dedicated to Gene Sherman who shaped my life even in his absence.

The poem "Heartland Home" is dedicated to Tamara Herendeen.

The poem "You Can't Win a Rodeo Sittin' in the Bucking Chute" is dedicated to Ofer Batat, due to his keen memory and quirky sense of humor.

The poem "Discontent" was inspired by Allison Joseph's poem "Melancholia."

The poem "First Day" is dedicated to Erez Batat, who has taught me to slow down.

About the Author

Ever since Diane Sherman was a little girl, she wanted to experience as much as possible so she could better understand human experience. This led her to travel the world, to become an artist, dancer, to work in investment banking, to become a graphic design consultant, and finally to become a yoga teacher. She grew up in the San Francisco Bay Area and recently moved to Spokane, Washington, lured by the seasons and their rhythm. She lives in Spokane with her husband, Erez Batat. She currently teaches yoga classes and yoga workshops in the Bay Area and the Inland Northwest. She finds inspiration teaching men in a Spokane correctional center.

Diane has been writing in one form or another most of her life. This is her first poetry collection. Her work has appeared in *Alembic, Pisgah Review, Diverse Voices Quarterly, The Spokesman Review, The Cape Rock,* and *Sanskrit Literary Arts Journal.*